Selected Poems
by
Daniel L. Knight

To Asa and Nellie Popp — two great people who have meant very, very much to me — with warmest regards, Dan Knight

DORRANCE & COMPANY • *Philadelphia and Ardmore, Pa.*

Copyright © 1977 by Daniel L. Knight
All Rights Reserved
ISBN 0-8059-2481-7
Printed in the United States of America

Contents

crossroads	1
the execution of a dandelion	2
prayer *(to the omniscient)*	3
yesterday, today, tomorrow	4
the great gray masses	5
the indian	6
I do not think that they will sing for me	7
We kill our heroes	8
ambivalence	9
the paradox	10
the architecture of war	11
the heart of mankind	12
the strongest voice	13
and there shall be wars, and rumors of wars	14
whited sepulchres	15
life is a confrontation	16
survivors	17
who am I?	18
solitude	19
The cry of a newborn babe is the song of humanity	20
starlight	21
humility	22
beyond ourselves	23
brothers of Icarus	24

songs of the soul	25
love	26
the blacksmith	27
there is hope for us, you and me	28
the *Titanic*	29
to my lifelong love	30
philanthropy and the politics of nations	31
How do you say goodbye?	32
elegy to a dead tenor	33

Selected Poems

crossroads

Our lives are a succession of
 opportunities, of roads traveled
 and roads not taken.

We are guided perhaps not so much
 by the roads we choose, but
 by the paths we have never trod.

the execution of a dandelion

The grey-haired old lady
in the blue print dress
stands on her front lawn,
a sun visor over her eyes,
a trowel in one hand and
a basket in the other,
slowly, judiciously removing the
crabgrass from the cracks in the sidewalk,
banishing the dandelions and all the
other assorted noxious weeds
to be consumed by fire
in the public burning area,
where great rotting heaps of
discarded, uprooted plants
wait for their mass destruction
in the name of richly watered acres
of fertilized Kentucky bluegrass.

prayer
(to the omniscient)

I see, yet I am blind.
I hear, yet I am deaf.
I know, yet I do not understand.
I love, yet I am lonely.
I dream, yet in this world
I am the most hopeless of men.

Open the eyes of my eyes,
the ears of my ears,
the mind of my mind,
the heart of my heart,
and fill me with the courage
to believe in things that may never be.

yesterday, today, tomorrow

We live in a world where the present cannot exist
without the past and the future.

In this world, today is a grand apparition
drifting on the sea of infinity.

It is as permanent as tomorrow's dreams,
and as real as yesterday's tears.

the great gray masses

In the endless crush of day and night,
of good and bad,
of happiness and sorrow,
living each day as the beginning,
leaving each yesterday only to return to it
 tomorrow,
we quietly spend our innocuous lives,
we, the members of the great gray masses.

We sacrifice our ambitions in return for
 the predictability of an hourly wage.
We submerge our peace of mind beneath
 the ambience of material possessions.
We sell our souls for the security of
 passive anonymity.

We crucify our dreams.
We prostitute our imaginations.
We die before we are truly born.

the indian

Silently, the old Indian with two canes
walked down the railroad tracks,
following the freight train
that had delivered him
a few minutes earlier.

He dusted off his threadbare coat,
shook back his long white hair,
smiled a toothless smile, and
slowly walked into another time,
from another world.

I do not think that they will sing for me

I do not think that they will sing for me,
the voices from the silent starlit past,
chanting incantations from a dark
and dank, mysterious, lonely castle tower.

I have never heard a sound as harsh
as that of peaceful penitents in prayer,
singing to the moon, the sun and stars
before the cataclysmic end occurs.

My eyes are frozen by the chilling sight
of destiny in all its glory rare.
My ears behold the siren call of fate.
My Burnam Wood has come to Dunsinane.

The stars have closed their lamps, the night is dark,
and I await the languid evidence
of that which once had been but now is lost,
of that which silence now has come to claim.

We kill our heroes

We kill our heroes.

We murder the singer,
   when after years of taking us over the rainbow
   she stumbles over lyrics now and then.
We murder the comedian,
   when after giving of his zest for laughter
   his lifeblood is drained by leeches that engulf him.
We murder the actress,
   when after baring her body to us freely,
   we refuse to see her soul.

We kill our heroes.
And with them, like them,
we kill ourselves.

ambivalence

How can it be that we both love and hate?

Do we ever love without fear?
Do we ever hate without pity?

To know the nature of ambivalence
is to understand the nature of humanity.

the paradox

We must remain as children
in order to grow as adults.
We must keep our sense of wonder,
of newness, and of imagination.
We must dream dreams
that have never been dreamed,
and we must ask new questions
in places where answers
have long become accepted.
We must continue to question,
to love,
to explore,
reaching not only into the unknown,
but into the familiar as well.

the architecture of war

Wars are fought not because of race
   or politics,
but because of expedience
   and architecture.

It is easier to build a wall,
   than it is to build a bridge.

the heart of mankind

The heart of mankind
   is like the wind,
   temperate,
   unfettered,
   flowing,
   powerful,
   destructive,
   loving,
   unseen.

the strongest voice

We capture and destroy
  what we do not understand.
We are intimidated
  by rivers undammed,
  by mountains unclimbed,
  by meadows unplowed.
We accept the idea that
  the only permanence in life
  is the assurance
  that all things change.

The screams of change,
  of tomorrow,
  of progress,
  have deafened our ears.

In our world of strangled peace,
  the strongest voice
  is the voice of silence.
It will take its rightful place,
  in time.
But there will be none left
  to hear its message.

and there shall be wars, and rumors of wars

We remember what we feel.

We forget what we have been forced to learn,
and have never experienced.

We become prisoners of the past,
and victims of the future.

whited sepulchres

I have been acquainted with musicians
who play only the notes on a page,
coldly, accurately, unemotionally,
as though they were a peculiar kind of
useful machine,
mindless reproducers of sound
playing only what is printed on the score before them,
seeing only the skeleton of the composer's anguish,
touching only the blueprint of the composer's dream,
never sensing the true music that lies
beneath the symbols on a page.
They have at their hands the magic of Bach,
of Brahms, of Beethoven, of Chopin;
yet they never know the wonder
that lies in the living, breathing soul
of that which they turn into
pious, repetitious monotony.
They, above all others on this earth,
are to be pitied.

life is a confrontation

Life is a confrontation,
   a battle between that which is
   wonderfully warm and serene,
   and that which is
   frighteningly violent and painful.

The result of this confrontation,
   this battle of the spirit,
   will tell the greatness of each soul.

survivors

We are all survivors
of the conflicts of life,
and the many minor tragedies
that occur in the cycle
of human existence.
Each day is a reiteration,
a recompense.
Each morning brings
a resurrection;
each night brings
a death,
a purgatory.
With each dawn we are
again reborn,
and with each sunset
we draw closer to the death
that awaits us every day.
Life becomes a succession of
little funerals,
a merry-go-round
of sweet dreams
and of bitter tears,
where each moment,
once past,
is gone like the fragrance
of the first rose of spring,
and the first love of a man's heart.

who am I?

You ask,
  Who am I
  to say these things?
  What do I know of life?

I reply that
  I am
  no greater than you,
  and no less. I know very
  little of life. I know only of
  that one small portion of it within me.
  But I know that one small portion very well.

solitude

At night I find my greatest freedom,
surrounded by sweet darkness and solemn dreams,
refreshed by the stillness of the night air,
released from the blinding harshness of unforgiving light
and the well-defined images of places and people,
filled with the lament of the night owl,
and the calm assurance of the moon.

**The cry of a newborn child
is the song of humanity**

The cry of a newborn child
  is the song of humanity.
    It says
      I hurt,
      I'm afraid,
      I'm cold,
      I'm hungry,
      I'm dirty;
      soothe me,
      hold me,
      warm me,
      feed me,
      cleanse me,
      for I am a stranger
      who has struggled
      into a new and
      different land.
      I am confused,
      and the way is hard.

starlight

Starlight is a fleeting,
glimmering message
from the past
written on the somber face
of the eternal present,
a remnant of things
that once were,
at once temporal and eternal,
forever lost,
yet forever reaching
into the cosmos,
into the limitless,
into the unknown.

humility

The ground
must be
broken
before
the seed
can be
planted.

beyond ourselves

In order to know ourselves
we must reach beyond ourselves.
For it is within the boundary
of our weaknesses
that we find the true
measure of our strengths.

brothers of Icarus

They are doers of deeds,
seekers of truth, and
renegades on the seas of time.
They leap headlong
into the winds of life,
soaring higher than eagles,
endlessly searching for rising currents
to lift them even higher,
in exhilaration daring to confront the sun,
knowing that in doing so
they seal their watery fate,
doomed to plummet like a meteor
into the turbulent ocean below.
Those who choose to fly higher than others
expect nothing more from life in return.
The gruesome end brings on no awesome fear.
The things they see are more than reward enough.

songs of the soul

Life is a symphony composed
   of all that we know as true.
It is the outward reflection of
   the elusive inner being,
   the quiet music within us.
We must sing the songs that are
   truly ours,
   not the songs of
   another person's dreams,
   another person's time.
We each must make of our lives
   our own symphony of life,
   so that when we meet,
   we touch each other
   with the themes that are truly ours,
   warm,
   living,
   knowing,
   human,
   immortal.

love

Love is the name given
  to the mystery
  that binds two people together.
Love is a wise old woman,
  it is an innocent young child,
  it is a star,
  it is moonlight,
  it is two souls,
  separate yet forever bound.
It is two halves who,
  until their meeting,
  were lost voyagers
  on the sea of tomorrow.

the blacksmith

In the toolbox
there is an old chisel,
its head unworn by repeated blows,
its blade unmarred,
as keen now as on the day it was made.
It was shaped at the forge
of a man who would accept
nothing less than the best he had within him.
The blacksmith's life stands as strong today
as the quality of his painstaking work,
and the strength of his unremitting will.

there is hope for us, you and me

There is hope for us, you and me,
for as we love we are transformed,
and our love becomes the seed from which
all that is beautiful is grown.

Our lives become a beautiful garden,
a peaceful paradise,
an oasis in a barren desert
of sunbaked pain and windswept loneliness.

the *Titanic*

The man who sails pretentiously
on the ocean of truth
will someday drown in it.

to my lifelong love

You are gentle moonlight on a
   quiet summer evening.
You are the song that the young bird sings
   to the newly rising sun.
You are the promise of spring,
   when the death of winter
   seems much too permanent.
You are the softest, most peaceful,
   most loving gift that has ever been,
   is now, and ever shall be.

philanthropy and the politics of nations

When the solutions to the problems of people,
   the feeding of the starving,
   the relief of the suffering,
   the healing of the diseased,
are left to politicians,
   the poor again become victims,
   the hopeless become pawns on the
   chessboard of world affairs,
   and the pain and suffering of
   helpless thousands becomes an
   internationally marketable commodity.

How do you say goodbye?

How do you leave behind
  all you've loved,
  all you've hated,
  all you've known,
without accepting the fact that
  those you've loved,
  those you've hated,
  those you've known,
will continue
  loving,
  and hating,
  and knowing?

elegy to a dead tenor

This is the finale ultimo,
the haunting last gasp of sound and song.
We sing, we cry, we scream,
knowing that when it ends—
the last note—
all that will remain is an echo,
hollow,
lonely,
languorous,
speaking of what we once were,
what we once dreamed,
softly fading,
settling gently as the fine dust of death,
until the gnawing silence becomes
the proof of our existence,
the essence of our lives.